★ IT'S MY STATE! ★

New Mexico

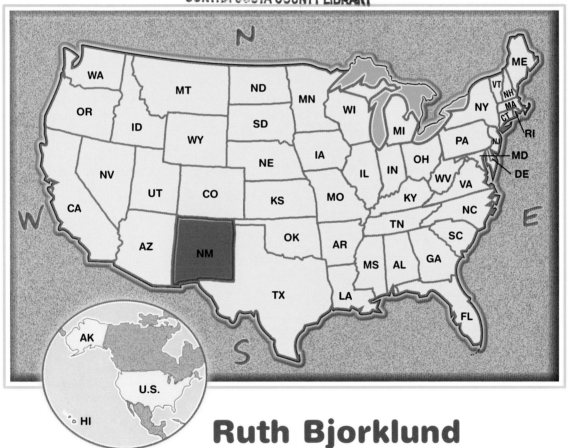

Ruth Bjorklund

BENCHMARK BOOKS

MARSHALL CAVENDISH
NEW YORK

Series Consultant

David G. Vanderstel, Ph.D., Executive Director, National Council on Public History

*With thanks to Rose Diaz, Research Historian, University of New Mexico General Library,
Political Archives, for her expert review of the manuscript.*

Benchmark Books
Marshall Cavendish
99 White Plains Road
Tarrytown, New York 10591-9001
www.marshallcavendish.com

Library of Congress Cataloging-in-Publication Data

Bjorklund, Ruth.
New Mexico / by Ruth Bjorklund.
p. cm. — (It's my state!)
Summary: Surveys the history, geography, economy, and people of New Mexico.
Includes bibliographical references (p.) and index.
ISBN 0-7614-1526-2
1. New Mexico—Juvenile literature. [1. New Mexico.] I. Title. II.
Series.
F796.3 .B56 2003
978.9—dc21
2002015073

Photo research by Candlepants, Inc.

Cover photograph: Paul Chesley/Stone/Getty Images, Inc.

Back cover illustration: The license plate shows New Mexico's postal abbreviation, followed by its year of statehood.

The photographs in this book are used by permission and through the courtesy of: *Corbis*: 27, 32, 33, 46 (top), 46 (middle), 66; Dave
G. Houser, 4 (top), 72 (top); Buddy Mays, 4 (bottom), 75; Adam Woolfitt, 9, 59, 71, 73 (top); David Muench, 11, 15 (top); Tom
Bean, 12, 13; Kevin Schafer, 14 (top); D. Robert & Lorri Franz, 14 (middle); George D. Lepp, 14 (bottom); Joe McDonald, 25 (bot-
tom); Larry Neubauer, 22; Bettmann, 24, 30, 35 (bottom), 46 (bottom); Michael T. Sedam, 36; Macduff Everton, 42; Craig Aurness,
45; Hulton-Deutsch Collection, 47 (top); Tony Roberts, 47 (middle); Catherine Karnow, 49, 72 (middle); Danny Lehman, 50, 52;
AINACO, 53; Lowell Georgia, 54; Liz Hymans, 56; Craig Lovell, 58; Wolfgang Kaehler, 62; Robert Holmes, 4; Roger Ressmeyer, 67;
Richard A. Cooke, 68; Marc Muench, 70; Reuters NewMedia Inc., 72 (bottom); Charles E. Rotkin, 73 (middle); Kennan Ward, 74.
Nancy Crampton: 47 (bottom). *Animals Animals*: Ray Richardson, 4 (middle); E.R. Degginger, 5 (top); Donna Ikenberry, 15 (mid-
dle); Joe McDonald, 16; Charles Palek, 17; Paul & Joyce Berquist, 19. *Chuck Place / PlaceStockPhoto.com*: 39. *Mark E. Gibson*: 73 (bot-
tom). *Getty Images*: Burke/Triolo Productions / FoodPix, 5 (middle); Harvey Lloyd / Taxi, 8; Paul Chesley / Stone, 38, 48; Brian
Hagiwara / FoodPix, 43. *PictureQuest*: Gene Peach / Index Stock Imagery, 44. *Hulton / Getty Images*: 31. *Photo Researcheres, Inc.*:
Francois Gohier, 5 (bottom). *Courtesy Museum of New Mexico*: Neg. No. 27986, 20; Emil Bibo / Neg. No. 44817, 29; Neg. No.
11409, 35 (top). *Smithsonian American Art Museum, Washington, DC / Art Resource, NY*: 23.

Book design by Anahid Hamparian

Printed in Italy

1   3   5   6   4   2

Contents

A Quick Look at New Mexico

Nickname: Land of Enchantment
Population: 1,819,046 (2000)
Statehood: 1912

Flower: Yucca

The yucca is a spiky plant with a white flower on the end of its 2-foot stalk. Native Americans used the roots to make soap. "Soapweed" is one of the yucca's local nicknames.

Bird: Roadrunner

Known as the chaparral bird, the roadrunner is a desert bird that feeds on insects, lizards, mice, and snakes. It would rather run or walk than fly. Able to race at speeds up to 15 miles per hour, the roadrunner is quick enough to chase and devour a rattlesnake.

Tree: Piñon Pine

Piñon (PEEN-yon) pines grow slowly. They reach up to 35 feet in height. Their root system below ground is equal in depth. The piñon is prized for its sweet smell and tasty seed, the pine nut.

Insect: Tarantula Hawk Wasp

The tarantula hawk wasp can be metallic blue, with red or orange wings. Before the female lays her eggs, she captures, stings, and paralyzes a tarantula spider. Then, she lays her eggs on its body. Once they hatch, the young wasps use the tarantula as their food.

Vegetables: Frijoles and Chiles

The New Mexico legislature declared frijoles (free-HO-lays) and chiles the state vegetables. In the sixteenth century, Spanish settlers brought frijoles (pinto beans) and chiles (spicy red or green peppers) to New Mexico. They have been key ingredients in the state's diet ever since.

Fossil: *Coelophysis*

Coelophysis *(see-loh-FIE-sis) was one of the first dinosaurs on Earth. It lived about 210 million years ago. This meat-eating dinosaur was about 9 feet long, with a pointed head, jagged teeth, and three claws on each hand. Its name means "hollow form," because its bones were hollow. Scientists discovered hundreds of* Coelophysis *in a bone bed near Ghost Ranch, New Mexico, in the 1940s.*

NEW MEXICO

Rocky Mountains

Wheeler Peak

Bisti Badlands

Taos

Kiowa National Grassland

Los Alamos

Santa Fe

Chaco Canyon National Monument

Albuquerque

Rio Grande River

International UFO Museum

Roswell

Pecos River

Gila Wilderness

White Sands National Monument

Gila River

White Sands Missile Base

Carlsbad Caverns National Park

Las Cruces

N

W   E

S

1 Land of Enchantment

New Mexico is a land of natural wonders. From soaring mountains to deep, dark caves, from vast golden deserts to red canyon walls, the land glows under dazzling skies. Author Charles Lummis wrote, "Most of New Mexico, most of the year, is a . . . harmony of browns and grays, over which the enchanted light of its blue skies casts an eternal spell . . ." Let's take a look at this enchanting place New Mexicans are proud to call home.

New Mexico's Borders
North: Colorado
South: Texas and Mexico
East: Oklahoma and Texas
West: Arizona and Utah

The Landscape

New Mexico is the nation's fifth-largest state. Yet it can seem that the 121,593 square miles are still not enough to hold all of the state's variety.

New Mexico's landscape is extraordinary. The majestic Rocky Mountains tower over the northern part of the state, while the vast prairies of the Great Plains cover eastern New Mexico. The mighty Rio Grande (Spanish for "big river") flows north to south through the center of the state. In other parts of New Mexico there are more mountain ranges, mesas (broad, flat-topped rocks with cliff-like sides), canyons, valleys, caverns, rivers, and arroyos (dry riverbeds that fill with water when it rains or when snow melts).

The Rocky Mountains and the Great Plains

The southern end of the Rocky Mountains covers northern New Mexico. The Rio Grande flows through the range and splits it into other ranges, such as the Sangre de Cristo Mountains. This is where snow-covered Wheeler Peak rises. Over 13,000 feet high, it is the tallest point in the state. In New Mexico's mountains you will see canyons,

The Four Corners region is the place where Colorado, Utah, Arizona, and New Mexico meet. Each state is one corner.

Sangre de Cristo means "blood of Christ" in Spanish. When the sun begins to set, the mountains turn blood red.

Often called the backbone of the state, the Rio Grande was vital to the Native Americans and the European settlers who first came to New Mexico.

ancient lava flows, and high mountain meadows. Nearby, you will also find cities and towns, such as Los Alamos, Taos, and Santa Fe.

Grasslands cover New Mexico's Great Plains region. Short, hardy bunchgrasses such as blue grama and buffalo grass grow as far as the eye can see. The southeastern section is called *"El Llano Estacado,"* which means "staked plains" in Spanish. Some say the term comes from Spanish explorers who long ago pounded stakes in the ground to mark their routes. With an average of five people per square mile, it is a remote land of open spaces and vast ranches.

> *New Mexico . . . was great, and splendid. . . . The landscape lived, and lived as the world of the gods.*
> —English novelist D. H. Lawrence

More than a hundred years ago, ranchers began raising cattle and growing crops to feed them. The cattle stripped the prairie of its grasses. In times of drought the grass would not grow, cattle could not eat, and farms failed. In New Mexico's Kiowa National Grassland, the U.S. Forest Service bought the farms and tried to replant the prairie. The grass did not grow as well, so the Forest Service turned to a biologist named Allan Savory. Savory said a healthy prairie needed the buffalo. He noted that when wild buffalo fed on prairie grass, they stayed in herds, ate the grass to the ground, and stomped on what they did not eat. The trampled grass turned into sod, a rich soil. Cattle do not usually graze the same as wild buffalo. So Savory suggested that the cattle should be fenced together so that they too could trample the prairie grass. It worked! Native grasses and wildflowers that have not bloomed in decades now flourish in the Kiowa National Grassland. "I love the land and its wildlife," writes Mr. Savory.

The Intermountain Region

The intermountain region covers southern, central, and western New Mexico. There are several ranges, including the Zuni, Mogollon, Cibola, Sandia, Guadalupe, and San Andres Mountains. Many of these ranges are named after Native American tribes. The Rio Grande brings life-giving water from the Rocky Mountains all the way to Mexico. Other rivers, such as the San Juan, the Gila (HEE-la), and the Pecos nourish a variety of plant and animal life. In other parts of the region there are high mesas, badlands, caves, canyons, and rock formations. Near the Pecos River, you will find Carlsbad Caverns, one of the most famous cave systems in the world. Its Big Room is the largest underground chamber in North America. If you visit, try and stay until sunset. As the sun starts to go down, hundreds of thousands of Mexican free-tail bats stream out of the caves. Scientists say the bats can eat 11 tons of insects on a summer night!

World Heritage Sites are special cultural or natural sites chosen by the United Nations. These sites are considered among the most important in the entire world. The Great Wall of China and the Pyramids of Egypt are some examples. New Mexico has *three* World Heritage Sites: Carlsbad Caverns, Chaco Canyon, and the Taos Pueblo.

Carlsbad Caverns' cave system was created over millions of years. Water dripped from the mountains, wore down the rocks, and left strangely shaped mineral deposits.

Two other unusual places are the eerie White Sands Desert and White Sands Missile Base. Billions of tons of a white mineral called selenite, or gypsum, form miles of dunes. Dunes are mounds of sand that pile up when the winds blow.

Western New Mexico has many wilderness areas. The country's first national wilderness is among them. The Gila Wilderness, part of the Gila National Forest, is where ancient people once lived in cliff dwellings. It is also a land of dry mesas, steep canyons, and badlands. From the rock formations called the Bisti Badlands in the northwestern corner of the state, you can travel 700-year-old roads into Chaco Canyon. There, ancient people built a huge city in the canyon walls. When you visit

Through the years, wind and water created Bisti Badlands' bizarre rock formations.

Chaco Canyon, you can still see the remains of their amazing accomplishment.

The Climate

The climate of New Mexico is generally mild, sunny, and dry. The average rainfall is 13 inches per year. Winters are drier than summers. Temperatures and precipitation (the amount of water the area receives) vary widely from day to night, from summer to winter, from mountain to valley, and from north to south. The south gets about 8 inches of rainfall each year. But in the north, it is closer to 30 inches. "No matter what," says a woman from Taos, "the rain is always welcome."

In winter, cold air moves south from Canada and brings snow to the mountains, and occasionally snow, rain, or hail to the valleys. Year-round average temperatures are 50 to 60 degrees Fahrenheit. But they can rise to 100 degrees in the summer and below 0 degrees Fahrenheit in the winter.

Taos artist Georgia O'Keeffe wrote that New Mexico is "more sky than earth." In summer, brief, heavy thunderstorms are common. New Mexico has more lightning strikes than any other state. As one resident says, "The lightning is absolutely terrifying; it's so right there in front of you. We just stay inside until it's over." When thunderclouds pour rain, the arroyos fill and often create dangerous flash floods. But in dry regions, the thunderclouds bring more wind than rain, stirring the dust into tornado-like swirls called dust devils.

Storm clouds brew over the plains of El Llano Estacado.

New Mexico's summer thunderstorms are the power of the land. . . .
—Photographer Ansel Adams

Plants & Animals

Agave

For its first thirty years, the agave grows a clump of tough, stiff leaves that store food and water. Then, using the stored nutrients, a flower stalk appears. It grows nearly a foot per day for two weeks. Flowers bloom, giving off scents that attract insects and bats. Soon after flowering, though, the plant dies. Native Americans ate the roasted stalk or used it to make flutes. Agave was also used in making rope, rugs, baskets, and cloth.

Javelina

The javelina, or collared peccary, is the only native wild boar in the United States. Javelinas have large heads with piglike snouts, slender legs, and a sharp, straight tusk. Their name comes from the Spanish *javelina,* which means "javelin" or "spear." They feed at dawn and at dusk and are fond of prickly pear cactus.

Pika

The pika, also known as the cony or rock rabbit, is part of the hare and rabbit family. It looks like a guinea pig. The pika lives in high, rocky places and is known for its squeaking and screeching sounds. When no other animals are around, the pika dashes from its den and grabs mouthfuls of grass. It lays the grass in the sun, building little haystacks that it will store for winter.

Prickly Pear Cactus

The prickly pear cactus has sharp yellow or red spines all over its flat, fleshy pads or leaves. The pads hold water and many desert animals seek the plant for this stored fluid. Some people cut off the spines and prepare the pads as a vegetable called nopales. Native Americans once mashed the cactus to use it as a medicine to heal wounds, and as an ingredient in glue.

Turkey Vulture

The turkey vulture soars overhead looking for animals that have recently died. Its Latin name means "purifier" because the vultures rid the countryside of decaying animals. The turkey vulture is brown with a red, featherless head that resembles a turkey's. Unlike other birds they have a keen sense of smell. In some cases, engineers have used turkey vultures to sniff out gas leaks in pipelines.

Western Banded Gecko

At night, this desert lizard hunts for insects, spiders, and baby scorpions. After a good meal, the gecko cleans its face with its tongue. It stores extra food as fat in its tail. If a predator should step on that tail, it will snap off. But the banded gecko can grow a new one.

Wildlife

Throughout the state you can find many different types of plants and animals. The forests in New Mexico's mountain regions are lush with pine, fir, aspen, and spruce trees. Clear

streams and lakes are filled with Rio Grande trout. Roaming freely in this high country are elk, mule deer, bobcats, and mountain lions. You may also see coyote, bighorn sheep, and bears. The black bear is the official state mammal. These creatures roam the state's woodlands, eating berries, nuts, fruits, plants, and wild animals. Black bears have coats that can be either brown or black, and they can weigh from 200 to 600 pounds.

The people of the Santa Clara Pueblo regard the black bear as a symbol of good luck because the bear always knows how to find water—a useful skill in the dry areas of New Mexico.

Mountain lions—also known as cougars or pumas—can weigh more than 150 pounds.

New Mexico's deserts and canyons are filled with cactuses and other plants that thrive in the hot and dry conditions. Lizards, snakes, spiders, scorpions, and small rodents scamper across the dusty ground. In the sky, eagles and hawks soar in search of prey. The climate presents a challenge to some nesting desert birds. They do not always sit on their eggs to keep them warm. Sometimes they will spread their wings above their nest to block the sun and keep the eggs cool.

Along the Rio Grande, near the Bosque del Apache National Wildlife Refuge, hundreds of thousands of birds gather. They include tropical songbirds, raptors (birds of prey), and giant sand-hill cranes. Lucky bird-watchers may even catch a glimpse of endangered species, such as the American whooping crane, which they fondly call a "whooper."

New Mexico's plants and animals are an important part of the state. Many residents try to help the state's wildlife in a number of ways. They conserve resources such as land and water, protect the animals' natural habitats, and make sure that threatened or endangered animals are not hunted. At Gray Ranch, in part of southwestern New Mexico, farmers, ranchers, the U.S. Forest Service, and conservationists joined forces to protect more than nine hundred species of plants, mammals, reptiles, amphibians, and birds. Some are threatened or endangered such as the Shirakawa leopard frog, the New Mexico ridge-nosed rattlesnake, Baird's sparrow, and the white-sided jackrabbit. Peter Warren of the Nature Conservancy said, "The spirit of what's going on here is that people are trying to get

We believe in wilderness, because that's where our hearts and souls are.
—Vicente Lujan Sr., Taos Pueblo

At a height of five feet, the whooping crane is the tallest bird in North America.

together and . . . make some progress toward solving some of our mutual problems . . ." Around the state, people are working to live in harmony with the land.

2 From the Beginning

Long before Europeans set sail for North America, great civilizations thrived in the land that is now called New Mexico. In spite of the rugged landscape, early humans lived in harmony with the earth, just as present-day New Mexicans live in harmony with the ways of the past.

The Old Ones

Twelve thousand years ago, New Mexico's first people roamed the grasslands hunting bison, mammoths, mastodons, and antelope. They made tools and weapons out of stone. But eventually the climate became drier. Many of the large animals died or left in search of food. So the people—ancestors of today's Native American people—started a new way of life. They hunted smaller animals and gathered nuts and berries. After a time, they built cities out of dried mud and stone and began growing crops such as corn, squash, melons, and beans.

Two of these ancient groups were the Mogollon in southwestern New Mexico and the Anasazi in the north. The

These children lived in Santa Fe in 1915.

The remains of the circular kivas are still visible in this Anasazi village in Chaco Canyon.

Mogollon made pottery and built round houses in pits in the earth. They faced a central plaza. Each village also included a *kiva*. A kiva is a circular room with a central fireplace used by men and boys for worship or rituals. Usually made of adobe—sun-dried bricks formed from clay, water, and straw or grass—it is often entered only by a ladder through a hole in the roof. Kivas still exist in ancient ruins throughout New Mexico and can be found in many present-day Native American villages.

The Mogollon were expert farmers. They also built irrigation ditches and traded with the Anasazi. The Anasazi were mainly basket makers and hunters and gatherers. But they soon learned farming and pottery making from the Mogollon. The

Anasazi used stone and adobe to build extraordinary towns, plazas, kivas, and cliff dwellings. Their largest city was in Chaco Canyon. Chaco was an important site for trading as well as a cultural and religious center. Hundreds of hand-laid stone roads lead into Chaco. Small bands of Anasazi families built

The word *Anasazi* is from the Navajo language, meaning the "old ones" or "enemies of our ancestors." Today, some prefer to use the term *Ancient Pueblo people* when speaking of the Anasazi.

houses that can still be seen along these roads. These simple villages are called "Chaco outliers." As a Taos photographer says, "Chaco is simply magical."

By 1600, the Anasazi and Mogollon civilizations mysteriously disappeared. Many believe these ancestor tribes left their villages because water became scarce. They probably joined with other native cultures. Today's Pueblo people are their descendants.

Other native groups, such as the Navajo and the Apache, moved from Canada to New Mexico. In the beginning these tribes were nomadic. This means that they

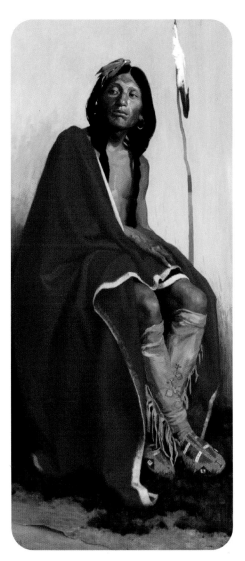

Elk-Foot, the Pueblo Indian shown in this painting by Eanger Irving Couse, is probably a descendant of the Anasazi and Mogollon people.

moved from place to place, following buffalo herds and hunting for food. When hunting became harder, Pueblo villagers feared the nomads because they raided their villages for food and other supplies. Eventually, the nomadic tribes settled into their own villages and began farming. Today, the country's largest Indian community, the Navajo Nation, covers part of New Mexico.

The name *Navajo* comes from a word used by other tribes to describe where the Navajo lived. It means "large planted fields." In their own language, the Navajo call themselves *Diné* (Dee-NAY), meaning "the people."

The Spanish Enter

Not long after the Navajo and Apache moved into New Mexico, Spanish explorers arrived. They had conquered the Native Americans of Mexico and made the area into a Spanish colony.

Cabeza de Vaca and his men traveled through the deserts of New Mexico but never found the fabled cities of Cíbola.

The Spanish then continued moving north, searching for gold, silver, gems, and other treasures to send to the king of Spain.

The first fortune hunter in New Mexico was Álvar Núñez Cabeza de Vaca in 1536. He had heard stories from the native people about the Seven Cities of Cíbola, which were cities thought to be so rich that the streets were lined with gold. Cabeza de Vaca never found Cíbola, and he returned to Mexico City. But other explorers still dreamed of finding riches in the lands to the north. In 1540, Francisco Vásquez de Coronado ventured one thousand miles into the Great Plains. He reported to the king of Spain, "[It] troubled me greatly, to find myself on these limitless plains, where I was in great need of water, and often had to drink it so poor that it was more mud than water." But the lure of riches sent more of his countrymen north on El Camino Real, "the royal road," into the land they called New Mexico. As Spanish soldiers, settlers, explorers, and priests came upon the humble native villages made of mud, they called them pueblos after the Spanish word for "town."

When the Spanish came across a Pueblo village, they assigned it a patron saint. There are nineteen Pueblo tribes in New Mexico. Many villages have kept their saint's names such as Santa Clara, San Juan, and San Ildefonso.

The Spanish had two reasons for exploring this "New World": finding treasure and spreading the Roman Catholic faith. At first, the native people were friendly toward the newcomers, but the Spanish proved to be terrifying. The Indians had never seen men on horseback. Some were frightened by the gleaming swords the Spanish carried as weapons.

The first Spanish colony in New Mexico was near the Rio Grande, north of present-day Santa Fe. Four hundred settlers led by Don Juan de Oñate established *haciendas,* or ranches. The settlers found it difficult to farm the dry land and forced the Indians to work the fields. Oñate built Catholic missions throughout the region, and priests tried to make the Indians practice Christianity. The Spanish burned kivas, destroyed sacred objects, and challenged Indian religious leaders. Oñate's soldiers were so brutal that he was eventually sent back to Mexico City in disgrace. Spain wanted to abandon New Mexico completely, but the priests refused to leave behind the Indians who had become Christians. So Spain declared that New Mexico would be missionary land.

In 1609, the Spanish returned with a new governor, Don Pedro de Peralta. He moved the capital city and named it Santa Fe. Despite the new leader, the relationship between the Spanish and the Native Americans did not improve. The Indians resented working on the haciendas, tending the mission gardens, wearing European clothing, and being forced to accept a religion other than their own.

By 1680, the Pueblo had had enough. A religious leader of the Tewa Pueblo people named Popé led the only successful revolt by natives in the New World. Pueblo leaders sent runners as messengers to the many communities to inform them of the planned revolt. Every community leader received a knotted rope. Each day, the leaders untied a knot. When all the knots were gone, the Indians knew it was time to fight. They surrounded the Spanish settlements and forced the Spanish to withdraw. Afterward, Popé ruled New Mexico for many years. But the Spanish returned in 1692, led by Don Diego de Vargas. For more than a hundred years after the Indians' victory, Spain controlled New Mexico.

The Americans Appear

In 1821, New Mexico celebrated Mexico's independence from Spain. At first, there was little change in the region's day-to-day life. But when the new rulers of Mexico opened the country's northern borders, American traders and travelers poured in. They established the Santa Fe Trail from Missouri and brought new trade goods to New Mexico. These included clothing, candles, books, furniture, and knives.

In 1846, the United States declared war on Mexico. A U.S. general named Stephen Kearny led his troops into New Mexico and declared New Mexico American territory. Two years later, the countries agreed to a treaty that gave New Mexico to the United States.

New Mexico was new to the United States, but when the Civil War began in 1861, the future state played an important

Many traders, and later settlers and their families, braved the Santa Fe Trail in search of new business and new lives.

role. Both the Northern and the Southern armies wanted New Mexico on their side. After New Mexico sided with the Union Army of the North, it won the support of most of the Great Plains.

In the mid–1800s, Americans of northern European descent, known as Anglo-Americans or Anglos, moved into New Mexico. They came to find new homes, adventure, and gold. Warrior tribes, such as the Apache, Comanche, Kiowa, and Navajo had bitter feelings about the Anglos invading their lands. Battles between U.S. soldiers and Native American warriors such as Geronimo and Cochise marked decades of bloodshed. In 1864, the U.S. government sent Kit Carson to handle the problem. Carson was a trapper and a scout who had friends among the Indian tribes. Still he followed government orders and forced the Navajos to walk 300 miles across wintry northern New Mexico to a reservation on the eastern plains. Many died during this tragic march, which was known as the Long Walk. Slowly more native groups were moved from their lands. The Indian Wars in New Mexico ended when Geronimo surrendered for the Apaches in 1886.

By the time the Anglos came, the Pueblo and the Hispanic settlers had inhabited New Mexico together for more than two hundred years. As farmers and ranchers, they had banded together for protection from the raids of other tribes. They intermarried and learned to share and accept each other's culture. But the Anglos brought a new culture and way of life. After the Civil War, the Anglos took over the government and made new laws. Many Anglos taught school or worked with the railroads. Before long, the Anglos had achieved positions of power in many New Mexican communities.

The New New Mexico

New Mexico had once belonged to Mexico and Spain. But in the nineteenth century, it became part of the lively American West. The territory filled with cattle, cowboys, railroads, miners, gunslingers, gamblers, and adventurers. Cattle ranching became big business as new railroads made it easier to transport cattle to eastern markets. But the sudden growth led to conflicts. Cattle ranches needed water, and landowners argued over water rights. In Lincoln County, a feud between cattle ranchers turned into a long and bloody war. One local gunfighter, nicknamed Billy the Kid, became a legend. He was celebrated in poems, songs, and even a symphony.

Laying railroad tracks across the dry plains of New Mexico was very hard work, but the railroad brought prosperity to the state.

These Pueblo children lived in Santa Clara in the early 1900s.

In 1850, New Mexicans asked to enter the Union as a state. But politicians in Washington, D.C., were unsure. They had heard shocking stories about Indian wars, cattle rustlers, and gunfighters. They did not trust New Mexicans. One reason was because many New Mexicans' primary language was Spanish. So most voted against making New Mexico an official part of the nation. A congressman from New Jersey defended the New Mexicans, saying, "Spanish Americans of New Mexico were Americans by birth, sympathy and education, furnishing more troops to the Union army during the Civil War than some of the new states." But there was little talk of statehood until the Spanish-American War of 1898, when President Theodore Roosevelt asked New Mexican gunfighters to join the Rough Riders. This was a band of soldiers who helped to free the island nation of Cuba from Spanish rule. New Mexicans again displayed their courage and loyalty. A frontier doctor declared that one New Mexico soldier was a "hero worth a hundred ordinary soldiers . . . ready to subsist [survive] on snakes, rats, and saddle leather without a whimper. . ." Despite proving their loyalty over and over, New Mexicans still had to wait. They were not granted statehood until January 6, 1912.

Changes Big and Small

In the early 1900s, doctors in the East started sending patients to New Mexico for the warm weather and the clean, dry air. Artists, writers, photographers, and tourists came and were struck by the region's beauty. In a letter from Santa Fe, the photographer Ansel Adams wrote, "This is a place to work—and dream."

Along with the people who came for adventure or better health were those who wanted to make a living off the land. Mining companies dug for copper, silver, lead, gold, and other minerals. Gas companies drilled for oil and natural gas. In remote areas, the U.S. military established airfields, military outposts, and laboratories.

This family worked together to make a living on their farm in Pie Town in 1940.

Navajo code talkers memorized the entire code and used it while under fire on the battlefield. Without these soldiers' skills, many battles would have been lost.

New Mexicans have long been active in the U.S. military. During World War I, the brand-new state sent troops to battle in Europe. The state offered even more troops at the outbreak of World War II. One noteworthy unit was the Navajo code talkers, a part of the U.S. Marines. From 1942 to 1945, these highly trained soldiers used their native language to deliver secret messages to U.S. soldiers on the battlefield. The Navajo soldiers were chosen because their language is unique and difficult to translate. At the time, only people who grew up speaking Navajo were familiar with it. The enemy never broke their code.

The Manhattan Project was another New Mexican military achievement. The purpose of the project was for U.S. scientists

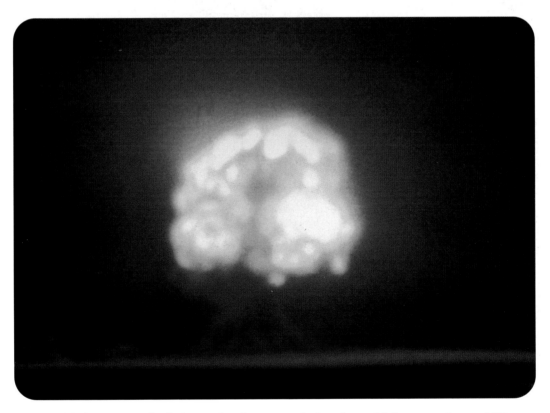

The reddish-orange flash from the first atomic bomb could be seen almost 150 miles from the test site.

to secretly develop the first atomic bomb. This weapon is a powerful bomb that gets its strength from the energy given off from splitting atoms—the building blocks of all matter. One of the chief scientists was Robert Oppenheimer, who had camped as a child in the remote mountains of northern New Mexico near the village of Los Alamos. He suggested they hide their laboratory there. When it was time to test the bomb, scientists chose a remote site near Alamogordo

The mineral trinitite is found only in New Mexico. It is a green material made of sand melted into glass by the heat of the explosion of the first atomic bomb. "It kind of glows," reports a local resident.

named Trinity. In 1945, they buried the first atomic bomb in a container deep in the sand. When they blew it up, it broke windows in houses 120 miles away. When the United States next dropped the bomb it was on Hiroshima, Japan, and led to the end of World War II.

At the end of the twentieth century, people moved to New Mexico to work in mining, government laboratories, ranching, and the oil and natural gas industries. Even when jobs are scarce, the population continues to grow. A lifelong resident of Las Cruces remarks, "People just trickle in on the Interstate. First they leave California, and then they find Phoenix, Scottsdale, Tuscon, and here. But when they get here, they stay." After looking at New Mexico's past, you cannot help but admire those who fought for the right to stay, to live, and to work in this extraordinary land.

Important Dates

10,000 B.C.–8,000 B.C. Prehistoric humans hunt mammoth and bison.

A.D. 1–1300 Anasazi people make baskets, weave cloth, and build elaborate stone structures at Chaco Canyon.

300–1300 Mogollon people farm and create pottery.

1200–1500 Pueblo people establish villages along the Rio Grande.

1536 Cabeza de Vaca crosses into New Mexico looking for the Seven Cities of Cíbola.

1540–1542 Coronado explores the Southwest and the Great Plains.

1598 Don Juan de Oñate establishes the first Spanish settlement.

1680 Popé leads the Pueblo Revolt, forcing the Spanish to leave New Mexico.

1692 The Spanish return, led by Don Diego de Vargas.

1807 Zebulon Pike leads the first Anglo-American expedition into New Mexico.

1821 Mexico declares independence from Spain and New Mexico becomes a province of Mexico.

1821 The Santa Fe Trail opens.

1846 The United States declares war on Mexico.

1848 Mexico gives New Mexico and California to the United States in the Treaty of Guadalupe Hidalgo, ending the Mexican-American War.

1863 New Mexico is divided in half, creating the Territory of Arizona.

1863–1868 Navajos and Apaches are moved off their native lands and onto reservations where thousands die of disease and starvation.

1886 Geronimo surrenders, and the Indian Wars end.

1912 New Mexico becomes the forty-seventh state.

1924 The first national wilderness is established at Gila Wilderness.

1945 The first atomic bomb is exploded at the Trinity site.

1946 The first rocket to leave Earth's atmosphere is launched from White Sands Missile Base.

1948 New Mexico's Native Americans are granted the right to vote.

1998 New Mexico celebrates its cuartocentenario, commemorating the four-hundredth anniversary of the first Spanish settlement.

Don Diego de Vargas

Robert Oppenheimer

3 The People

New Mexican society is mostly based on three cultures: Native American, Hispanic, and Anglo. Through the centuries, these groups of very different people have sometimes disagreed. Yet over time, they have learned to share each other's customs and traditions. Today there are also growing populations of Asian Americans and African Americans in the state. But African Americans represent only about 2 percent of the population, and Asian Americans a little more than 1 percent. The three primary cultures have played the

We are all peoples of this land
We were created out of the forces
Of Earth and Sky,
the stars and water. . . .
—from "The People Shall Continue"
by Simon Ortiz, Acoma poet

largest part in shaping the state so far. But regardless of their race, all New Mexicans are proud of their communities, which are rich with diversity and heritage.

In October the people of New Mexico fly balloons high above Albuquerque.

The Native People

Native Americans make up nearly 10 percent of the population of New Mexico, more than any other state. They are direct descendants of the original people who lived in the region. This gives them close ties to their ancestral lands and traditions. The state's three major groups are the Navajo, Apache, and Pueblo.

There are nineteen Pueblo villages. Though they share a similar culture, all Pueblo people do not speak the same native language. The people of each Pueblo village have a distinct art, craft, or means of making a living. Some people living in the Santa Clara, San Ildefonso, and Acoma Pueblos are potters. Many of the Isleta Pueblos are farmers. The Picuris are painters. Still others, such as the people of the Santo Domingo Pueblo and the Zuni, make jewelry. Today not all Pueblo people live in their

A mother and daughter use a traditional oven to bake bread at the San Ildefonso Pueblo.

While living in a hogan on the Navajo Indian Reservation in Shiprock, this Navajo woman weaves a rug with bold patterns and colors.

ancient adobe villages. Many live in nearby towns or cities. But for them, it is important to come home for celebrations and feast days.

The Apache and the Navajo also add to the state's blend of native cultures. Today many Apaches live on reservations. The Jicarilla Apache live in northern New Mexico and the Mescalero are found in the south. Known traditionally for basket making, most Apaches today work for the tribe's ranches, resorts, and mining operations.

The Navajo Nation has 16 million acres in the Four Corners region. Most of the reservation lies in Arizona, but a third of the Navajos live in New Mexico. Many families, or clans, trace their origins to Chaco Canyon. Navajos hold a variety of jobs, but many are weavers, silversmiths, farmers, and sheepherders. On a reservation you might see a Navajo hogan. Hogans are traditional Navajo buildings that are usually round or multi-sided. They are made of logs and are sometimes covered with earth. Although only a few families in remote areas still live in hogans, each clan has one for special ceremonies.

In a Navajo hogan the door always faces east toward the morning sun. Men sit at the south, women, the north, and visitors have a place of honor at the west. When entering, a person moves in a clockwise circle, following the path of the sun.

A Zuni Ring Game

In the past, Zuni children played a game using rings made from bent twigs covered with colored cord. Here is a version of the game you can play with slightly larger rings.

What You Need

Pencil

Four jar lids, glasses, or plates between 2 and 6 inches across. One lid should be at least 2 inches bigger across than the other lid.

Cardboard from notepad or cereal box

Scissors

Double-stick tape

Regular scotch tape

Medium-weight yarn, 4-6 yards each of blue, green, and white (traditional Zuni colors)

Trace around your largest lid on the cardboard and cut out the circle. Repeat with a lid at least 2 inches smaller in a new spot on the cardboard. Inside each circle draw a second circle using a smaller lid. Be sure to leave a rim about 1/2 inch wide. Cut out the inner circles and throw those pieces away. When cutting out the inner circles it is helpful to bend the cardboard gently to make your first cut in the middle of the circle.

Cover the two rings on both sides with pieces of double-stick tape.

Cut the yarn into 3-foot pieces. Push one end of the white yarn through the hole in the smaller ring and wind it around and around, covering the ring completely. When you finish, make a knot, cut off the extra yarn, and attach it to the ring with a piece of scotch tape. Be sure to tape it down smoothly so that the ring will lie flat on the floor. Next, wind the blue and green yarn around the larger ring. You can alternate the colors to create a pattern.

To play the game, place the big ring on the ground. Stand over it and try to toss the small ring so it falls within the big one without touching it. When this gets too easy, move farther back. Figure out a scoring system and have fun!

The Hispanic Tradition

Before the English established the first American colonies in the East, the Spanish had formed settlements in New Mexico. Spanish families in the Southwest have lived longer in what is now the United States than those who first settled in New England.

In colonial times, Spanish rulers gave their noblemen large land grants in Mexico and New Mexico. Landowners learned how to farm from the Pueblos and established farms as well as sheep and cattle ranches. They introduced two animals to the New World: the cow

New Mexico has a state question: "Red or green?" What it means is, "What color chile sauce would you like on your food?" New Mexico is one of the few states in the United States with a regional cuisine, or way of cooking. Using chiles, corn, beans, and squash as basic ingredients, New Mexican-style cooking has become world famous.

and the horse. Soon *vaqueros*, or cowboys, rode the plains, rounding up herds of cattle and driving them to market. The Spanish also introduced the Catholic faith, which is still practiced by many people throughout the state.

Ranching is still an important part of New Mexican life today.

Recipe for Guacamole

This is a simple recipe with delicious results. Guacamole has long been an important part of New Mexican cuisine. This dish is an example of how the Mexican culture has helped to shape the state's foods.

Ingredients:

2 large, ripe avocados
1 tomato
1 green onion
green chile
1-1/2 teaspoon fresh lime juice
1/4 teaspoon garlic powder
1/2 teaspoon salt

Ask an adult to help you prepare the ingredients for this recipe.

First, peel the avocados and remove the pits. Using a fork, mash the avocados together. Set the avocados aside while you prepare the other ingredients.

Cut the tomato, green onion, and chile into tiny pieces and mix these together. The amount of chile you use depends on how spicy you want your dip. But be careful because chiles can be hot!

Combine all of the ingredients together and squeeze in the fresh lime juice. Once everything is mixed well, it is ready to serve. Your guacamole can be used as part of other Mexican dishes, such as tacos or burritos, or eaten as a dip with tortilla chips.

Young New Mexicans perform traditional Mexican folk dances in Santa Fe.

Around 42 percent of New Mexico's population is Hispanic, or Latino. Some New Mexicans can trace their origins back to the noble families who were granted land by the Spanish rulers. Through the years New Mexican culture has been influenced by Spanish traditions and language. Across the state today you can still see businesses, communities, and events that share and celebrate the state's Spanish heritage.

The Anglos

The Anglos who made their way to New Mexico in the early nineteenth century showed spirit and courage. They came as miners, cowboys, ranchers, and adventurers. By the end of World War II, many other Anglos moved to the state to enjoy the warm climate and peaceful environment. Today they are the state's largest ethnic group.

Part of the cowboy tradition stays alive when men and women compete in rodeos across the state.

Famous New Mexicans

Geronimo: Apache Leader

Geronimo's true name was Goyathlay, or "One Who Yawns." After his wife and children were killed in a Mexican Army raid, he swore revenge. He attacked with such fury that he made the frightened Mexican soldiers cry out to their patron saint, San Geronimo (St. Jerome). Geronimo took that as his warrior name. He fought against the U.S. and Mexican Armies and became the last Indian leader to surrender to the U.S. government.

Georgia O'Keeffe: Painter

Georgia O'Keeffe was born in Wisconsin but later moved to Ghost Ranch, New Mexico. Driving around in her Model T Ford, O'Keeffe would see a subject, stop the car, and set up her paints and easel on the side of the road. Her paintings feature desert flowers, adobe churches, and animal skeletons.

William Hanna: Cartoonist

William Hanna was born in Melrose, New Mexico. He studied to be an engineer, but he loved to draw cartoons and soon moved to Hollywood. There he paired up with another cartoonist, Joseph Barbera. As the team Hanna-Barbera they won countless awards for their cartoons. They are responsible for creating Tom & Jerry, Huckleberry Hound, Yogi Bear and Boo-Boo, Quick Draw McGraw, Scooby Doo, the Jetsons, the Flintstones, and many more.

Conrad Hilton: Businessman

Conrad Hilton was born in the small farming town of San Antonio, New Mexico. Hilton used to meet travelers at the station and carry their baggage to the local hotel. He went on to buy and build Hilton hotels around the world. When he died, he left his huge fortune to the Conrad N. Hilton Foundation, a charity he established to help children, promote world peace, and support Catholic nuns who work with the poor.

Nancy López: Professional Golfer

Nancy López was born in California but moved to Roswell, New Mexico, when she was young. She played her first game of golf when she was eight. By the time she was twelve, she had won the New Mexico women's amateur championship. She went on to win so many golf titles so quickly that she became the youngest golfer ever admitted to the Ladies' Professional Golf Association (LPGA) Hall of Fame.

Leslie Marmon Silko: Writer

Leslie Marmon Silko is a New Mexican poet and writer of Pueblo, Mexican, and Anglo heritage. She grew up in the Laguna Pueblo reservation and uses traditional storytelling styles in her novels. She said that she learned to tell stories because in her community "children belong to everybody and the way of teaching is to tell stories. . . . It is easier to remember that way."

The Arts

New Mexicans are very proud that their state is the third-largest producer of art in the world, after New York and Paris, France. Nature and tradition often inspire New Mexican artists. The people of the Santa Clara Pueblo feel that they are part of the earth. They use the same word *nung* to mean both people and clay. Pottery made in pueblos such as Cochiti, Santa Clara, Acoma, and San Ildefonso are collected by museums around the world.

Native American jewelry makers are known for their fine work in silver and turquoise. Navajos use wool from their sheep to create highly prized rugs and blankets. The Apache are known for their elegant handmade baskets. Traditionally, New Mexico's Indians painted with sand or on rock. Today, many blend old ways with modern styles to create unique works.

In the early part of the twentieth century, Anglo artists from New York and Europe visited Taos and Santa Fe. There, they painted the striking landscape. The best known was Georgia O'Keeffe, who declared, "All the earth colors of the painter's palette are out there in the many miles of badlands . . ."

A gift shop in Taos displays and sells the rugs, blankets, and pottery produced by the local people.

In architecture, Spanish and Pueblo designs are combined to create what is called Santa Fe style. It features houses formed out of earth-colored adobe. Wood timbers, called *vigas*, form the framework and poke through the adobe. On the inside, an adobe fireplace is often in the corner and bold Navajo rugs cover clay tile floors. While these houses are very attractive, they are also very practical. The adobe and tile keep the houses cool in summer and warm in winter.

Music has also been a strong part of New Mexican culture. Music lovers from around the world gather under the stars at the open-air Santa Fe Opera House to listen to classical music. Native Americans use music in their ceremonies and celebrations. The most famous symbol of New Mexico is the humpbacked, flute-playing Native American god, Kokopelli, who serves his people as a magician, musician, rain priest, and song carrier. The Spanish and Mexicans brought mariachi music, salsa, and folk music to the state. Anglos brought European folk songs and cowboy ballads.

A fiddler plays traditional country music at the Hatch Chile Festival.

Having Faith

The British novelist D. H. Lawrence said the religion of New Mexico's Native Americans was "a vast old religion, greater than anything. . . ." The spiritual lives of Native Americans is tied closely to nature. They celebrate their faith in kivas, in dances, and festivals honoring the natural world. The Navajo have a ritual called the Blessing Way. A singer performs to remove evil or fear, to protect people and animals, or to ask for an agreeable life. Sometimes, a Blessing Way song lasts for several days.

When the Spanish arrived and converted many of the Pueblos, the Indians kept many of their rituals, but added elements of the Catholic faith. For example, traditional dances such as the Corn Dance or Deer Dance are now held on a Christian saint's day. After watching a Taos Pueblo ceremony on San Geronimo Day, D. H. Lawrence said, "Never shall I forget the deep singing of the men at the drum, swelling and sinking, the deepest sound I have ever heard in all my life, deeper than thunder, deeper than the sound of the Pacific Ocean. . . ."

Spanish priests spread their religion throughout New Mexico. Catholic churches and missions in New Mexico are particularly beautiful, with adobe walls, folk paintings, carvings, and white crosses that stand out against the deep blue sky.

People of other religions have also found a home in New Mexico. You will see Jewish temples, Mormon temples, Protestant

During the Christmas holidays, many buildings and roads in New Mexico are decorated with luminarios *or* farolitos, *which means "little lanterns" in Spanish.*

churches, and East Asian ashrams, the religious buildings used by many Hindus. The country's only adobe Islamic mosque is located in New Mexico.

Problems for the Future

New Mexico is not a wealthy state in terms of income (the money that is made through work). There are jobs in the cities, but not enough for everyone. In the past, Hispanics and Native Americans were farmers and ranchers. Those skills are needed less in today's economy. So more Hispanics and Native Americans are living in poverty. Many cannot afford to live in decent homes or buy basic items. Sometimes they cannot even afford to buy enough food to feed the whole family.

To make matters worse, wealthy, mostly Anglo, newcomers have moved to cities such as Taos, Santa Fe, and Las Cruces to build vacation or retirement homes. Prices for land and housing in these areas have gone up because these people are able to pay higher amounts. As a result, some native New Mexicans can no longer afford to stay in the cities and towns where their parents once lived. Many believe that the newcomers have taken away their land. This often causes problems between these two different groups.

But New Mexico has a long multicultural history. New Mexicans know how to blend many ways of life to build a society that tries to represent everyone. Former U.S. congressman Steve Schiff believed, "Despite some differences, New Mexicans on the whole deal with racial and ethnic diversity much better than the rest of the country." Senator Jeff Bingaman thinks so too, stating, "I think most New Mexicans would agree . . . our state is a shining example of what's right."

Calendar of Events

Gathering of Nations Powwow

Each April in Albuquerque, more than five hundred tribes from the United States and Canada come together to share their cultures. Activities include dancing and the Indian Traders Market, which has Native American art, artifacts, traditional foods, and other items on display and for sale.

Clovis Pioneer Days and Rodeo

Every June in this eastern New Mexican city, you can enjoy parades, rodeos, concerts, and horse shows and sales. The event celebrates the history of the first farmers and ranchers who lived in the state.

Tour of the Gila Bicycle Race

In May, racers from around the world come to the high, rugged Gila Wilderness to test their mountain biking skills. Cyclists can compete in a variety of races, including some that span several days.

Zuni dancers

Roswell UFO Festival

Thousands of fans of science fiction and alien life-forms come to Roswell for its annual festival. This celebration marks the day in July 1947 when an alien spacecraft was believed by many to have crashed in a farmer's field. Roswell is home to the International UFO Museum.

New Mexico State Fair

The New Mexico State Fair is a harvest festival overflowing with ethnic foods, entertainment, arts and crafts, animal exhibits, car shows, and more. Held in Albuquerque each September, there is something for everyone at the fair. "I never miss the fair, it's the only time all year that I go to Albuquerque," says a woman from the town of Angel Fire.

Fiesta de Santa Fe

Late August brings the nation's oldest celebration, the Fiesta de Santa Fe. The festival includes fireworks, traditional foods, costumes, and dances. You can even watch the annual burning of Zozobra or "Old Man Gloom." Zozobra is a 40-foot paper puppet that symbolizes bad luck. Crowds cheer as flames make the puppet crumple. It is believed that once it is burned, everyone gets a fresh start on life.

Hot-air balloons

Hatch Chile Festival

The little town of Hatch doubles in size during the chile harvest. Lovers of spicy foods come to town to taste the newest chile crop. The festival is held on Labor Day Weekend.

Albuquerque International Balloon Fiesta

For ten days every October, one of the world's largest hot-air balloon and gas balloon events takes place. More than five hundred colorful hot-air balloons float in New Mexico's blue skies.

Festival of the Cranes

Each November during their migration, the sandhill cranes stop at the Bosque del Apache National Wildlife Refuge. New Mexicans celebrate the return of the cranes and other wildlife with arts and crafts, music, stargazing, and of course, bird-watching.

4 How It Works

For more than three centuries, New Mexico had governors appointed by others—Spain, Mexico, and Washington, D.C. Not until 1912 were New Mexicans able to elect their own government officials.

New Mexico, the State

Since New Mexico became a state it has used the constitution that was drafted in 1911. The laws in the constitution are similar to the U.S. Constitution, including a bill of rights. But unlike the federal Constitution, New Mexican politicians added a phrase making both English and Spanish official languages.

The Palace of Governors in Santa Fe housed governors for nearly three hundred years. Today a new state capitol is used. It is a round building designed to look like a kiva. It has four entrances that stand for the four winds, the four seasons, the four directions, and the four stages of life: infancy, youth, adulthood, and old age.

Santa Fe is the oldest capital city in the nation. It was founded in 1610.

An old wooden cart stands on display at the Palace of the Governors in Santa Fe. The palace now serves as a history museum.

There are three levels of government in New Mexico: municipal, county, and state. New Mexico has thirty-three counties. People elect commissioners to run county government. Within these counties there are ninety-three cities, towns, or villages. These are called municipalities. People living in these areas elect councils and sometimes mayors to run their local governments. They meet with these lawmakers to discuss issues in town meetings.

The highest level is the state government. Voters elect legislators, a governor, judges, and other executive officers. Citizens also vote for people to represent them in national government. Each citizen may vote for president, two U.S. senators, and one U.S. representative. New Mexico has three members of the U.S. House of Representatives. New Mexico is called a bellwether state in presidential elections. This means that New Mexican voters almost always choose the winning candidate.

New Mexico is mostly evenly divided between the Republican and the Democratic parties. State and county

This statue representing the Earth Mother stands in front of the state capitol.

New Mexico

Branches of Government

Executive In the executive branch, the governor, lieutenant governor, secretary of state, and other officers are elected to four-year terms. The governor is the head of the state. His or her duties include preparing the state budget, suggesting new laws, and choosing cabinet members and other department heads. He or she must also sign bills into law or reject them.

Legislative The legislative branch is made up of forty-two senators and seventy representatives. Each citizen can vote for one senator and one representative. Senators represent several towns, while representatives govern just one or two. Senators are elected to four-year terms, and representatives serve for two. Members of the legislature also form committees to discuss future bills.

Judicial The Judicial branch is a system of courts made up of a supreme court, the court of appeals, district courts, magistrates, and county and municipal courts. The highest court in the state is the supreme court. It oversees the actions of other courts and rules on the most serious criminal cases. District courts make decisions on serious crimes and lawsuits. The other courts rule on lesser crimes such as traffic violations. If there is a disagreement with a district court ruling, the case may be heard by the court of appeals.

officials are frequently Democrats, but federal representatives are more often Republican. A third party, called the Green party, is popular in the northern part of the state. The people of this party are concerned about protecting the environment and land and water rights.

The Federal Building in Santa Fe is made of adobe.

Nations within a Nation

New Mexico also has tribal governments. These governments are viewed as separate nations. Each of the nineteen pueblos, the two Apache tribes, and the Navajo nation has an independent government. They elect tribal councils. The head of a Pueblo government is called a governor. The Apache and Navajo each elect a president to head their governments. Tribal governments have their own constitutions that decide taxes, laws, fish and game rules, and religion. Pueblos also have an All-Indian Pueblo Council, which aids in governing common interests. These include environmental issues, education, and the Pueblo economy.

In 1948, Native Americans were given the right to vote in local, state, and federal elections.

Citizen Laws and Rights

The state constitution provides a set of laws that are the basis for New Mexico's government. One subject in the constitution is important to every citizen—water.

When New Mexico was a Spanish colony, the government granted certain people land and water rights. The Indians also had rights to water since ancient times. Because everyone had this same right, the state constitution made sure to describe how people could get and use water. The laws state that water running near your property is not necessarily yours. People often have to share the water with others. Landowner

A father and son walk past irrigation ditches that are used to water the lettuce crops.

associations built irrigation systems, or *acequias.* The irrigation ditches take water from the rivers and distribute it to people in the association. The more ditches that open onto your land or the closer you are to the opening of a ditch, the luckier you are. "The man who lives at the bottom of the ditch is forever disappointed," writes one acequia manager.

But with so many people in need of water, problems are unavoidable. The cities, such as Las Cruces, Santa Fe, and Albuquerque, are growing. With more people, the cities need more water, but the supplies are running out. So people want to take water from other places. Unfortunately, it usually comes from the rural farming communities

In 1620, Spanish governors made gifts of silver-tipped canes—called staffs of justice—to each Pueblo tribal leader. In 1863, President Abraham Lincoln also presented each Pueblo governor with a cane. It was the president's way of saying the United States recognized each pueblo as its own nation. Every January, when the new Pueblo governors take office, they each receive two silver-tipped canes.

that rely on acequias. Farmers, conservationists, and many lawmakers fear that once cities take someone else's water, laws will change and the small farmers will lose their water rights. The acequia associations have defended themselves in courts, saying their water rights are protected by the constitution. "Water is life," they cry.

How Laws Are Passed

Many New Mexicans care about the environment and want to protect it through tough laws. Several students, with help from their teachers, have joined a group called Wild Friends. Here is the story of how Wild Friends worked to pass a bill that protected wild animals from poachers—people who illegally hunt animals.

In New Mexico, only legislators can introduce a bill. So in 1997, two hundred students belonging to Wild Friends started writing letters, sending e-mails, and calling their legislators. They hoped that a representative or senator would sponsor, or introduce, their anti-poaching bill. They were very excited when the speaker of the house, Raymond Sanchez, agreed to sponsor their bill. All proposed bills are given numbers, so Speaker Sanchez's next task was to present the proposed bill to the chief clerk, who gave the bill the number 249. Then the bill was sent to committees for their approval. The speaker told the students the names of the representatives on the committees so that the students could begin writing more letters and e-mails.

When it was time to hold committee meetings, the students came with their teachers and parents to the state capitol in Santa Fe. They were allowed to speak out in favor of their proposal. They were nervous, but the legislators were very understanding. The students talked about how wild animals needed more protection from illegal hunters. The legislators listened carefully and took notes. After the meeting, the students went home and sent thank-you letters. Legislators say, "Thank-you notes go a long way!" The proposed bill then went to the next stage, which is a committee vote. The committee approved, so House Bill 249 was presented to the entire house of representatives. They also voted in favor of the bill. The bill then needed to go to the state senate. Again, it had to pass through committees, and again, the students wrote letters and e-mails and made trips to Santa Fe to testify. The committees, and then the senate, voted to pass the bill.

In New Mexico, as throughout the United States, every citizen has a right to speak his or her mind. These Native Americans are protesting the closing of casinos on tribal lands.

New Mexico

Here are some ways you can contact
New Mexico's state and federal lawmakers:
On the governor's Web site,
www.governor.state.nm.us
click on "Contact Form." It will help you e-mail the governor easily.
To find your state legislators go to
http://legis.state.nm.us/senate.asp
http://legis.state.nm.us/house.asp
The quickest way to look up telephone numbers and addresses or to e-mail
your U.S. officials is to enter your zip code on this Web site:
http://www.congress.org

Once the anti-poaching bill had passed both houses, it was sent to the governor for him to approve or veto. He decided to sign House Bill 249, making the Wild Friends's bill a law. Speaker Sanchez is quoted as saying that he is "very proud of all the students who participated. . . . I felt great knowing that I was helping teach some of our young people their first real lesson about government and the legislative process." The senate majority leader, Tom Rutherford, agreed with Speaker Sanchez, saying, "We appreciate what you Wild Friends are doing. You are making a real big difference!" He is right, and it is a key part of New Mexico's government that allows anyone, of any age, to get involved and make a difference.

5 Making a Living

New Mexico's ancient peoples built extraordinary cities, hauling blocks of stone on their backs over long, rugged roads. Later, their descendants constructed elaborate water systems to nourish their fields. Today, New Mexicans still have a close tie to the land and its many gifts.

Manufacturing

Manufacturing in New Mexico is different than in other states. There is no history of factory buildings, smokestacks, or conveyor belts. Instead, manufacturing is about new technologies and ancient arts.

New Mexico's economy was once based on farming and ranching. Since the 1940s that has changed and technology has become more and more important. During World War I and World War II, the United States needed to build up its military. In Los Alamos, hidden in the remote Jemez Mountains, and near Albuquerque, in the Sandia Mountains, the government set up top-secret laboratories to research and experiment with

Chile peppers are an important crop in New Mexico.

A Patriot missile is launched at White Sands Missile Range.

nuclear weapons. One hundred twenty miles away, on the White Sands Missile Range, the military tests nearly every rocket and weapon that the nation uses.

The government moved many scientists to New Mexico, and after the two wars, they stayed and worked on other projects, such as computers, robots, and energy production. Today, at the Sandia National Laboratories center in Albuquerque, scientists are designing one of the world's smallest robots. It is only one-fourth of a cubic inch and uses three tiny watch batteries. Scientist Ed Heller says it could be "the robot of the future." This robot might be able to do dangerous tasks such as finding gas leaks or cleaning up after disasters.

Miles from the nearest town, twenty-seven dish antennas, each more than 150 feet high, line the railroad tracks. From a distance, claims British writer Henry

Some important members of the White Sands Missile Range team are not human. Before launching test missiles, scientists spray the missile's parts with shark liver oil. After the missiles return to Earth, "missile dogs" are sent out to pick up the scent of the oil. They sniff over the rangeland and find the fallen rocket parts.

Shukman, they seem to be a "fleet of white sailing boats." In a way they are. But these giant dishes sail the cosmos. By using radio waves instead of light waves, the dishes give scientists regular information about solar systems a thousand light years from Earth. This National Science Foundation installation in the plains of New Mexico is the Very Large Array (VLA) telescope. With its dish antennas, the Very Large Array can

Each dish antenna is 81 feet in diameter and weighs 230 tons.

magnify something as small as a dime sitting on the moon. There are ten VLA telescope sites across America, from the U.S. Virgin Islands in the Caribbean Sea to Hawaii. They can all be connected to work together, to form the Very Long Baseline Array, the most powerful in the world.

Modern technology and prehistoric history joined in 1998, when the space shuttle *Endeavour* carried a skull of *Coelophysis*, the New Mexico state dinosaur, to the space station *Mir*.

Technology came to New Mexico in part because of its remote and open spaces. But today, most technology products are not made in secret. The government laboratories have helped industries start up in cities such as Albuquerque, Roswell, and Las Cruces. There, scientists and skilled workers make computer parts, medical equipment, and pharmaceutical products.

Another important form of manufacturing comes from the native peoples of the state. Native American arts and crafts have long been an important part of New Mexico's economy. In ancient times, Indian weaving, baskets, pottery, and jewelry were valuable trade goods. The same is true today.

Native Americans use turquoise in their jewelry and artwork.

Tourism

Tourism is New Mexico's largest industry. Visitors are drawn to the state's cultural variety. The Museum of Fine Arts has been around since before New Mexico officially became a state. The Museum of International Folk Art, near the Sangre de Cristo Mountains, shows arts and crafts from around the world. The Santa Fe Indian Market, held on a weekend in August each year, hosts around 100,000 visitors. Santa Fe chef Mark Miller says, "Indian Market is awash with color, sound, energy, and fragrances." On summer nights, the Santa Fe Opera House is filled with music lovers. Tourists also enjoy Native American ceremonies and Spanish fiestas.

Others visit New Mexico to see the rugged mountain ranges, deserts, canyons, and scenic rivers. They enjoy skiing, river rafting, fishing, hunting, and mountain biking. Skiers flock to Taos, Angel Fire, and the Mescalero Apache resort. In the Gila Wilderness, mountain bikers compete in international races. Says one Silver City resident, "I wouldn't *push* my bicycle up some of the hills those folks pedal!" Another outdoor activity in New Mexico is the Albuquerque hot-air and gas balloon festival. Locals insist you should never pass it up, "The balloons are awesome," says Agnes Gibson of Eagle's Nest.

Some of New Mexico's residents are unsure if the tourist industry is truly good for the state. Sometimes it seems to those already there as if too many visitors decide to stay. A resident comments, "Everyone who moves here, wishes they were the last. But then they miss their modern conveniences. People here in Angel Fire are afraid it will get crowded and be nothing but traffic jams!" Some people believe too many newcomers will harm the balance of nature. Yet others believe that income

This professional skier takes off from a cliff on a clear day in Taos Ski Valley.

from tourism keeps a special way of life alive. Albuquerque Mayor Martin Chavez agrees, saying "It is economic vitality which gives us the means to preserve our natural and cultural riches, the habits of the heart."

Natural Resources and Mining

In 1539, Fray Marcos de Niza reported that New Mexico was "a land rich in gold, silver, and other wealth." Many Spaniards believed his words and came to the new province hoping to find riches.

Mining did not begin until the early 1800s, when the Spanish started to take copper from the hills in Apache territory in the southwestern part of the state. They later mined gold and silver, but to this day, copper remains the state's top metal. It is used in plumbing pipes and electrical wires. Every car built in America, for example, has

Turquoise is a blue-green gemstone that has been prized for thousands of years. It is found in the earth near deposits of copper. Other minerals such as iron make up the stone—the less iron, the bluer the stone; the more iron, the greener the stone will be.

more than 50 pounds of copper. Mining companies have agreed to clean up their waste, but it is not always easy. One former miner says, "Mining here has not had so glorified a history. . . . There's no way around it, some of the things the environmentalists say are true—mining is very unsightly. Devastating. But it is controlled, and, it has to be, it's a dangerous job. Our big shovels dig six dump truck loads at once!"

Other minerals mined are potash, used to make fertilizer; coal; manganese, a metal used in making steel; and uranium, a mineral that fuels nuclear-powered plants and submarines. The leading mining product in the state is petroleum. Natural gas is found in the state. The fuels help supply the nation's energy needs.

Copper mines are very important to the state's economy, but years of mining badly damaged the land.

Products & Resources

Dairy Products

The climate in New Mexico is ideal for dairy farming. In 2001, there were 1.6 million head of cattle in the state—nearly as many cows as people! On average, farmers have 1,200 cows in their herds. A Roswell cheese factory is the largest maker of mozzarella cheese in the country. It uses four million gallons of milk a day.

Chiles

Chiles have been grown in New Mexico for at least four centuries. In the last three decades, New Mexico has produced more chiles than any other state. After harvest, people hang strands of red chiles, called ristras, outside to dry. The beautiful, deep-red ristras are a feast for the taste buds and the eyes as well.

Laboratories

In central New Mexico, many high-technology laboratories are involved in scientific research. They work in areas such as energy, pharmaceutical products, nuclear weapons, human genetics, computers, and robots.

Copper

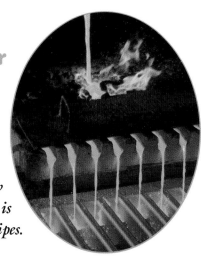

In 1800, an Apache warrior gave a Spanish soldier an arrow point made of copper. The soldier knew right away how important the metal was and went looking for its source. Copper has been mined in New Mexico ever since. The first copper taken out of New Mexico was turned into coins. Now most of the copper is used in making electrical wires and plumbing pipes.

Oil and Natural Gas

Most of the state's income from mining comes from oil and natural gas. Pipelines carry fuel to other states.

Tourism

Each year, more and more tourists flock to New Mexico to enjoy its scenic beauty, outdoor sports, arts and crafts, and cultural celebrations. Tourism has become New Mexico's largest industry.

Living on the Land

From the earliest Pueblo farmers, farming has been a New Mexican way of life. Crops include hay, corn, wheat, cotton, pecans, and chiles. In the dry northeast, farmers rely on deep wells and rainfall. Says one farmer's daughter, "When I visit my mom, I help her milk the cows. I don't know how she's done it all these years. Having to depend on rain, that's what makes it hard!" In other dry areas, people raise cattle on long-established ranches. In the rugged northwest corner, Navajos herd sheep.

But living off the land often creates problems. For years, ranchers have argued with concerned citizens about land and water use.

> Protecting the land is part of New Mexico's heritage. One famous symbol of this is Smokey Bear, a cub found in New Mexico in 1950. It was injured in a forest fire caused by careless people. The cub was rescued and lived a long life. A cartoon version of the cub still reminds us, "Only You Can Prevent Forest Fires!"

Cattle are allowed to graze on public land. But many people think cattle use too much water and destroy the grasses and soil. Ranchers say they have a right to protect their herds from attacks from wild animals such as wolves, coyotes, and bears. They also say elk eat crops meant for cattle. So, in cattle country, ranchers have killed off many of these animals.

Mexican gray wolves sometimes attack the livestock at ranches, but attacks on humans are rare and usually only occur when the wolf is sick or has no other food.

Another source of conflict has been the endangered Mexican gray wolf. Cattle ranchers drove away this creature a century ago. Recently, the U.S. Forest Service has reintroduced it in the Gila Wilderness. Farmers and ranchers are angry over the return of these wolves. "I can see both sides," says Rob Narvaez of the Gila Wilderness area. "I think the wolves can play a role and be a natural part of the ecosystem. But a lot of the pro-wolf people are not from here and they don't have the roots of the locals. Still, we all get together and we talk. The last time there was a meeting, we had to move, because we filled up the room!"

This struggle is not the first battle over how the land is used. But time and again, New Mexicans have proved that they can find solutions that preserve their values, culture, and traditions. As the New Mexico state motto proclaims, "It grows as it goes."

New Mexico draws on its traditions and its people to turn a bright face toward the future.

The state flag is yellow with the state emblem, the Zia, in red. The emblem is styled after the Zia Pueblo's symbol for the sun. The rays of the sun represent central elements of the natural and spiritual world. The rays are four groups of four lines that stand for the four directions, the four parts of the day, the four stages of life, and the four seasons. At the center is a circle, symbolizing life.

The state seal was adopted in 1912. In the center are two eagles: the large American bald eagle and the smaller Mexican eagle. The American eagle holds arrows in its talons, while the Mexican eagle has a snake in its beak, a reference to an ancient Aztec myth. Beneath both eagles is a scroll on which the state motto is written in Latin.

New Mexico

O, Fair New Mexico

Words and Music by Elizabeth Garrett

New Mexico also has an official song in Spanish entitled "Así Es Nuevo Méjico."

State Song

MORE ABOUT NEW MEXICO

Books About the State

Kent, Deborah. *New Mexico.* New York: Children's Press, 1999.

McDaniel, Melissa. *New Mexico.* Tarrytown, NY: Benchmark Books, 1999.

Of Special Interest

Anaya, Rudolfo. *The Farolitos of Christmas.* New York: Hyperion Books for
   Children, 1995.

Anderson, Joan. *Spanish Pioneers of the Southwest.* New York: E.P. Dutton, 1989.

Hoyt-Goldsmith, Diane. *Las Posadas: an Hispanic Christmas Celebration.*
   New York: Holiday House, 1999.

Pasqua, Sandra M. *The Navajo Nation.* Mankato, MN: Bridgestone Books, 2000.

Petersen, David. *Carlsbad Caverns National Park.* Chicago: Childrens Press, 1994.

Web sites

Official New Mexican Government Web site:

http://www.state.nm.us

Desert USA, an exploration of North American deserts:

http://www.desertusa.com/flora.html

Indian Pueblo Cultural Center:

http://www.indianpueblo.org

About the Author

Ruth Bjorklund lives on Bainbridge Island, a ferry ride away from Seattle,
Washington, with her husband, two children, two dogs, and two cats.
Some of her favorite memories are of travels through the enchanting state
of New Mexico.

Index

Page numbers in **boldface** are illustrations.